King Matt the First | Janusz Korczak

King Matt the First
Janusz Korczak

Translation from the Polish: Itzchak Belfer
Illustrations: Itzchak Belfer

Website: www.itzchakbelfer.com
Contact: itzchakbelfer@gmail.com

ISBN-13: 978-1717334671
ISBN-10: 1717334679

KING MATT
THE FIRST

JANUSZ KORCZAK

TRANSLATED FROM POLISH, ADAPTED AND ILLUSTRATED BY

ITZCHAK BELFER (A PUPIL OF JANUSZ KORCZAK)

CONTENTS

Preface   8

Heir to the Throne   10

At the Public Park   14

The Royal Gift   18

Writing Letters   20

A Secret Meeting   24

A Declaration of War   27

The Escape   31

They've Stolen the King!   33

The Revelation   38

King Matt's Solution   46

Epilogue   50

PREFACE

At the age when this photograph was taken, I wanted to do everything that was written in the book you are about to read. Later I forgot all about it. Now I am old and I neither have the time nor the energy to go to war or travel to the land of the cannibals...

My photograph appears here, because it is important for me to show how I looked when I wanted to be a king and not how I look today when I am writing about King Matt. I actually think that it is far better to see photographs of kings, explorers and authors when they are children, not grownups and old. One might think they were always wise and clever and were never little children. Children believe they may never become ministers, travelers or writers. That is not true, they can.

Janusz Korczak

HEIR TO THE THRONE

And so it came to pass...

The royal kingdom's Council of Ministers gathered in the Great Hall. They sat in their lush armchairs next to a long, well laid out table. In front of each minister was a sheet of paper and two pencils: one was ordinary, the other pencil had one point red and the other point blue. On the table in front of the Prime Minister, there was also a bell. The door to the great hall was bolted and locked so they would not be disturbed. The small table lamps before them were lit...and at first, no one said a word.

Finally, the Prime Minister rang his bell and declared, "We must decide what to do. The king is ill, and can no longer rule."

Then spoke the Minister of Justice: "When a king can no longer rule, the law decrees that the eldest son of the king shall rule in his stead. That is why he is called heir to the throne."

"But the king has but one son ..." said the Prime Minister.

"He doesn't need more than one." replied the Minister of Justice.

"True, but the royal prince, little Matt, cannot yet read or write, how can he be our king?" demanded the Prime Minster.

"The matter is simple," the Minister of Justice explained. "In our kingdom such a thing has never occurred, but in Spain, in Belgium and in other lands, it has happened that the king died and left a young son who by law had to be crowned king in his place."

"Right, right," popped up the Minister of the Post Office and Telegraph Service. "I myself have seen postage stamps with the likeness of a child-king of this kind."

Without delay, signs were put up on all the streets' walls of the kingdom announcing that little Matt was the new ruler of the land, that he sent his blessings upon all his subjects, and that he would be aided by his Council of Ministers in his reign.

Shop windows displayed pictures of young King Matt: riding a pony, dressed as a marine, wearing an army uniform, taking part in military parades. He was even shown in movie newsreels, and all the tabloids throughout the land and beyond its borders wrote about him and printed his picture... the truth is, everyone loved little King Matt. All the children in the land were very, very happy that one of their own was ruling the land and had to be obeyed by all. Even army generals stood at attention and soldiers had to present arms whenever he passed.

All the young girls in the land fancied little king Matt riding on his pony, but he was most loved by the orphan children because candies, games, and toys were sent to them from the palace in the name of their young King Matt...

AT THE PUBLIC PARK

King Matt, who was young and inexperienced in the ways of the world, had to ask permission from the royal physician responsible for him, to go to the public park where all the children played. "The royal gardens are the most beautiful in the kingdom, but I am alone, and I am weary of being by myself," sighed the boy-king.

After consultation with the King's ministers, the physician succeeded in getting permission for Matt to have three visits to the public park every two weeks. The young king was greatly pleased. He went dressed in ordinary clothes, so no one would know he was the king. And who would have thought a king would want to come and play in a public place anyway!? Matt circled the park twice and finally sat down on a bench near where the other children were playing. After a bit, a young girl came up to him and asked, "Would you like to play?" Immediately she took his hand and they played together. Later, between games, the girl started a conversation. "Do you have a sister?"

"No, I don't," he replied. "And what does your father do?" she asked, "My father...was the king."

The girl thought surely Matt was joking, so she laughed and said, "If my father were king, he would have to buy me a doll so big it would be as high as the ceiling!"

King Matt later learned that the girl's name was Irenka; that her father was captain of the fire brigade, and that she liked the firemen very, very much because sometimes they would let her ride on their horses.

Matt wanted to stay in the park longer, but the time allotted to him was up...and he had to leave.

The second time he went to the park, King Matt was playing with the girls in a circle, when suddenly a group of boys approached. One of them said, "Look, there is a boy here who is playing only with the girls!"

Matt saw that he was right – that he was the only boy in a group of girls.

"Would you like to play with us, too?" asked the boy.

Matt looked at the boy, whose name was Felek. Matt had noticed him before and wanted very much to get to know him. He had a feeling that they could be friends.

Felek looked closely at Matt and suddenly shouted, "He looks so much like King Matt!" Everyone burst out laughing.

At the next meeting of the Council of Ministers, it was decreed that the king could no longer be permitted to go to the park. They would grant whatever else he wished, but they could not allow him to go to a public park because there were uneducated children there who would laugh at him. The Ministers would not let their king be ridiculed and disrespected!

THE ROYAL GIFT

Half a year after the coronation of the king, something happened that led to his being held in great admiration. In other words, everyone spoke highly of Matt, not because he was the king but because he did something very special and very nice.

I will tell you how it came about.

King Matt was sad. He thought about the two visits he had in the park. Suddenly he remembered what Irenka had said to him: her dream was to have a doll as high as the ceiling. He could not get it out of his head.

"I am the king and it is my right to command," thought Matt, "but in the meantime, I do what everybody tells me. I'm learning to read and write like all the other children. I have to wash behind my ears, brush my teeth and do the same arithmetic problems everybody else does – the same problems for kings as for all children, so why am I a king?" He was furious.

In his next meeting with the head of the government, Matt loudly demanded that they buy the world's biggest doll and send it to Irenka. Matt remembered that once he had seen his father rock back and forth on his legs when he gave orders to the ministers, and now he did the same. Surprised, the head of the government looked at King Matt and wrote something down in his journal. "I will pass your demand on to the ministers at the next council meeting."

What was said at the meeting, no one knows, because it was held behind closed doors. Nevertheless, it was decided to buy the doll. The Minister of Commerce searched in all the stores for two full days, but he did not find any such doll as the king wanted. There was no choice but to have the owner of the shop fabricate a new doll, and this, at a great cost. When the doll was finished, the shop owner put it in his display window with the inscription: "The gift of King Matt to Irenka, daughter of the captain of the Fire Brigade". In the newspapers, they published a photograph of the Fire Brigade putting out a fire, and Irenka with the doll.

In the course of the next three days, large crowds came to the shop to see the royal gift. They disrupted the cars and trams, so that on the fourth day – on orders from the Chief of Police – the doll was removed from the display window so that traffic could flow without disturbance. For a long time after, people spoke about the doll, about Matt, and about Irenka, who received such a wonderful gift.

WRITING LETTERS

King Matt arose each morning at 7 o'clock. He washed his face and got dressed by himself; he shined his shoes by himself and made his bed by himself. He drank a small glass of cod liver oil, and sat down to breakfast – sitting by himself. Then he went down to the royal gardens, where he could run around and play for an hour. But it was not much fun playing by himself, so he was glad when it came time for his lessons. Matt studied hard, because he knew that if he did not get an education, it would make it difficult for him to be king.

One day, the thought popped into King Matt's head that when he learned how to read and write, he could write a letter to Felek and maybe Felek would write back, and in that way, it would be like talking to him. From that moment, Matt dedicated all of his time and energy to learning how to read and write. For days on end, Matt copied stories and poems from the books in the royal library. King Matt, who was bright and determined, said to himself: "In another month I will write the first letter to Felek." Although it was difficult, he continued his writing exercises, and after a month – without anyone's help – the letter to Felek was ready.

Dear Felek, I have been watching you happily playing in the public park for a long time, and I would very much like to play together with you. However, I am the king and I cannot. I like you very much. Write to me and tell me about yourself, because I want to get to know you. If your father is serving in the army, perhaps they might let you come to the royal gardens sometimes...

Signed, King Matt

Matt's heart was pounding when he called out to Felek at the fence to the public park and gave him the note he had written. His heart beat even more wildly the next day when Felek gave him a note in the same manner.

Your Highness,

My father is a sergeant in the Royal Guard. I would be very happy to come to the royal gardens. I am ready sire, to go through fire and water for you, to defend you to the last drop of my blood. If you should need my aid, just whistle, and I will come immediately.

Felek

Matt hid the letter in a drawer. He knew he had to be cautious; he did not want anyone to know about Felek, because if he asked for Felek to be allowed in the royal gardens, they would start asking questions, like: "How come? Where does this Felek come from? How did you meet him?" And what if in the end they don't allow Felek to enter the royal gardens?!

A SECRET MEETING

In the meantime, I will learn to whistle, decided King Matt. It is not at all easy to learn to whistle if you do not have someone with you who can show you how to do it. Nevertheless, King Matt was determined to teach himself to whistle. One day, when he was in the royal gardens, he tried out a whistle, and to his surprise, in front of him stood Felek, as tense as a violin string, standing at attention. "How did you get in here," asked the surprised King Matt.

"Over the fence," replied Felek. In the royal gardens tall raspberry bushes grew. King Matt and his friend crouched down behind the bushes, discussed between them what they should do, and how they should continue.

"I am a very miserable king, Felek," said Matt. "Since the minute I learned how to write I have been signing papers and decrees, and that means that I rule all the land. But I do whatever I am told to do, and it's very boring. They don't let me do anything that's fun."

"But who can give you orders, your highness?" Felek asked. "Before, I did what my father told me to do," said Matt, and now it's the ministers who tell me what I have to do all the time, and what I can and can't do." "Before, you were the heir to the throne but now you are the king!" said Felek.

"That's true, but now it's a hundred times worse because there are so many ministers." "Are there cherries in the royal garden too?"

The question surprised Matt, but he replied that yes, there are cherries in the royal garden, and pears, too, and he promised Felek he would pass him as much fruit as he wanted through the fence.

Felek was pleased, but then he became serious and said, "We won't be able to meet very often, because they might see us. We'll pretend we don't know each other. We'll write notes to each other and put them on the wall. When you want to pass me a letter – whistle and I'll come right away and get it."

"And when you send me your letter in reply, you whistle," said King Matt. "It's forbidden to whistle at the king!" said Felek in the utmost seriousness and added, "I can make the sound of a coo-coo bird." "Fine," Matt agreed happily. "And when will you come again?"

Felek thought for a long while and answered, "Without permission I can't come. My father is a sergeant and he doesn't allow me to come near the fence of the royal gardens. He warned, 'Remember I am your father, and if they catch you there, you will get a very harsh punishment,'" "So how will you get home now?" Matt asked him worriedly.

"After your royal highness goes, I will find a way," said Felek. Matt parted from Felek and made his way between the bushes just in time, as his courtier had been searching for him all over the gardens.

A DECLARATION OF WAR

From that day on, King Matt and Felek worked together. Often, King Matt complained to his royal physician about his loneliness. But the physician only weighed Matt and measured his height once a week to see when little King Matt would be big King Matt...

King Matt asked the Minister of War to teach him how to march. The minister agreed immediately and said he would bring up the request at the very next council of ministers meeting. But at the next council meeting the ministers were concerned with only one subject. Three countries had declared war on King Matt.

When Matt and Felek met again in secret, Matt was very sad and worried because he was sure they would not allow him to go into battle. He was indeed, the king, but he was still a child. "Felek," cried Matt and took his friend's shoulder. "What I am going to tell you right now is secret. Don't betray me, remember!"

"As you command, your majesty."

"Tonight we will run away together to the front lines of the war!"

"As you command, your majesty."

"You will call me by name"

"As you command, your majesty."

"I am not the king now, I...wait, wait, what name should I choose for myself? I know! My name is Tomac!" decided King Matt.

The two friends decided that that very night – at two o'clock in the morning, they would meet by the fence of the royal gardens. "Tomac," said Felek, "if we go together, our food rations have to be bigger." "Right," said Matt, somewhat perplexed, because at such an important moment, it's not proper to think of one's belly...

THE ESCAPE

"Tomac, are you there?" called Felek at the hour of their nighttime meeting.

"Yes, I am."

"For gosh sakes, it's pitch black, we could bump into the royal guard, you need to hurry."

Matt was barely able to climb the tree, and from the tree on to the fence, and from there to jump outside the palace grounds. He hurried to catch up with Felek, afraid he would lose him in the dark. He was breathing hard; Felek wasn't walking, he was running hard. "Didn't you bring a coat?" Felek asked.

"No, my coat is in the royal clothes closet."

"You didn't even take a coat? To go to war like that is really childish," said Felek in all seriousness. When they got to the front, the scene that greeted Matt's eyes reminded him of the stories he had heard about war. There was a huge military encampment. Spread out over a large plateau were numerous small fires. Soldiers sat around each one, resting, talking amongst themselves, and drinking hot tea. The two tired friends stretched out next to one of the fires and slowly fell asleep.

In the early morning, Matt took a position in the trenches on the edge of the encampment. It was very quiet and pleasant sitting there, but suddenly and surprisingly, it began. First, small cannon shots were heard – barking, afterwards the big guns – roaring. Then finally, the sound of rifles – cracking. One popped here, another whistled there. The commotion lasted half an hour or an hour and then – quiet again. This was war.

THEY'VE STOLEN THE KING!

Now I must tell you what happened in the palace after they saw that **King Matt was gone...**

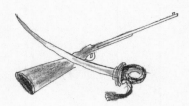

In the morning, the head household servant entered the king's bedroom and could not believe his eyes: the window was open, the bedclothes were rumpled, and there was no trace of Matt. The servant went immediately to the Minister of Ceremonies and said, "The King has disappeared."

The Minister of Ceremonies contacted the Prime Minister. Not ten minutes went by, and three official limousines pulled up to the palace drive, with the Prime Minister, the Minister of the Interior and the Commander of the police. "They've stolen the king!" said the Minister of Ceremonies. "Who else knows that the King is missing?" asked the stern-faced Minister of the Interior. "No one," replied the Minister of Ceremonies. "We must find out what happened to him," said the Minister of the Interior. "Commander", the Prime Minister turned to the commander of the police, "I order you to take care of the matter, and begin the search!" In the royal gardens, there was a fishpond. Perhaps Matt had drowned? They brought a diving suit from the royal navy and the commander of the police put a big rubber mask over his head and dove to the bottom of the pond. But Matt was nowhere to be found. The ministers decided to tell the people that Matt had taken ill and the royal physician told him to lie down in bed, so there would be no lessons for the king today. The presence of the royal physician served as proof that indeed this was the case.

"Today we can all appear calm," said the Prime Minister. "But what shall we do tomorrow?" "I'm the head of government and I have a head on my shoulders," said the Prime Minister. "Here's what we shall do," And he turned to the Minister of Commerce. "Do you remember the doll that Matt commanded we buy for Irenka?" "I remember it very well," replied the minister.

"Go, sir, immediately, to the same shop and tell the owner that he is to make the same kind of doll for King Matt by tomorrow. However, no one must know that it is a doll. Everyone must believe that the doll is King Matt. In the meantime, have posters put up in the streets, saying, "Citizens of the capital city can keep working during wartime," and his highness himself, King Matt, will ride through the streets of the city every day in an open car to encourage his subjects.

THE REVELATION

Meanwhile, Matt was injured in one of the battles on the front lines of the war. He was greatly upset to have to go to the hospital with a minor wound, but the field doctor insisted, and made him go anyway.

In the hospital, Matt slept on a mattress covered with a white sheet, a pillow and a blanket. It was the first time that Matt had slept in a bed since he ran away from the palace to go to war.

The days went by and slowly Matt healed from his wounds. The doctors and nurses were very kind to him, and he felt very good. But the possibility that someone on the hospital staff might recognize him made him uneasy.

One morning an elderly general entered his room.

"How is your majesty?" asked the general, and saluted.

"My name is Tomac, a simple soldier, sir general," Matt replied hastily.

"Really..." laughed the general. We will see about that right now. Call Felek!" And into the room walked Felek.

"Tell me, Felek," said the general. "Who is this?"

"This is his royal highness, King Matt the First."

Matt could no longer deny his identity, and actually, it would not have been right to do so. The opposite, things could not have continued this way, with a giant doll responsible for ruling the kingdom!

It was the general who told Matt about the doll they had made in his likeness, and how the doll was driven around each day in the streets of the city; how the Prime Minister placed the doll on the throne at royal audiences with the people, and how the doll, by their pulling its strings gently, would nod its head and salute. When the general had finished describing to Matt the situation in the kingdom, he went on to speak of more pressing matters.

"Can his majesty participate in consultations?" he asked Matt.

"Yes," replied Matt.

An officer then entered the room, as the general continued to tell about everything that had taken place during the war.

Three powerful kings had declared war against King Matt. The first one was defeated by Matt's army and was taken prisoner. Matt's army routed the second king and all his weapons were taken away so that he would not be able to wage war for a long time. Just the third king was left and he had not yet engaged Matt's army in battle. "Should we order the army to pursue the soldiers of the defeated armies?" asked the general. Everyone awaited for Matt to speak.

KING MATT'S SOLUTION

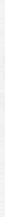

Matt was silent and thought for a while, until finally he asked, "Where is the king that was captured?"

"Not far from here," answered one of the officers.

"Bring him to me," commanded Matt.

And so they did. The captured king was brought to Matt in chains.

"Remove the chains," Matt ordered.

"Oh, king," Matt said to him. "I know what captivity is like; therefore, I am granting you your freedom. My armies defeated yours and I ask you to remove all foreign troops from my kingdom. Return all of you, to your land and to your homes. I promise I shall not pursue you.

The next day a signed letter was received from all three enemy kings: "King Matt, you are courageous, wise and generous. Why do we need to fight? We are returning to our lands and wish to be your friends.

Do you agree?"

Matt agreed and declared a union of peace.

King Matt arrived in the royal train back to his capital city and was greeted with great joy by the people.

A long limousine awaited him there, but Matt demanded they bring him a white stallion to ride. King Matt rode slowly through the streets of the city. From the windows of the houses many of his subjects watched him pass and they cheered him, but the ones who made King Matt the most happy of all were the children, who threw flowers and shouted with a loud voice, "Hurrah, hurrah, long live King Matt the First!!!"

EPILOGUE

One night, King Matt pondered long and hard, and devised a plan.

"The ministers shall continue to be in charge of matters to do with adults, and I shall be the king of the children and grow together with them. When I reach age twelve I will reign over all the children up to my own age. And when I am fifteen, I will be king of all the children up to that age. I myself will do all that is needed for the children like me."

***

Thus did Janusz Korczak tell us these tales at the orphanage. He meant that adults are locked within their own world and do not take the opinions of children into account, or even consider that they have the same rights as adults. Moreover, he believed that if one third of humanity are children, then we, the children, deserve a third of the world's natural treasures and resources. We, the children, know what is good for us, and we want a voice in the decisions that concern us and our fate. If the great leaders and ministers think they know and understand what is good for adults – that is all right, but for children, it is not all right.

***

Dear boys and girls, the story you have just read is but a small fragment of a larger work written by Janusz Korczak, entitled King Matt the First. A second book he wrote about King Matt is called "King Matt on the Desert Island."

I wanted you to know the beginning of an enchanted story, one that you will love. And when you grow up, perhaps you will read the entire book, even both books - because there are no stories like these in today's modern world! For example, in the book you will learn about Princess Clou-Clou and her adventures with King Matt in Africa.

If you wish to know more about the orphanage of Janusz Korczak, you can read about it in another book I have written and illustrated, entitled: The Man Who Knew How to Love Children.

Yours truly,
__Itzchak Belfer__

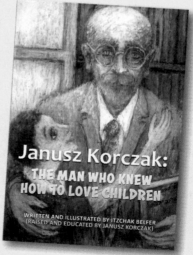

Made in the USA
Middletown, DE
09 May 2019